Chew Chew Chew

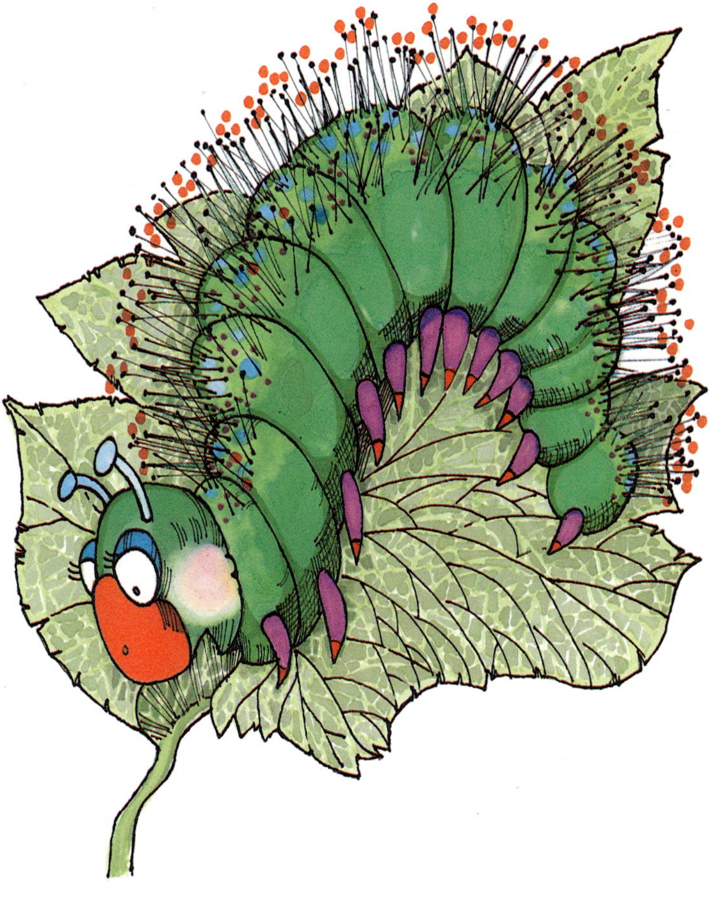

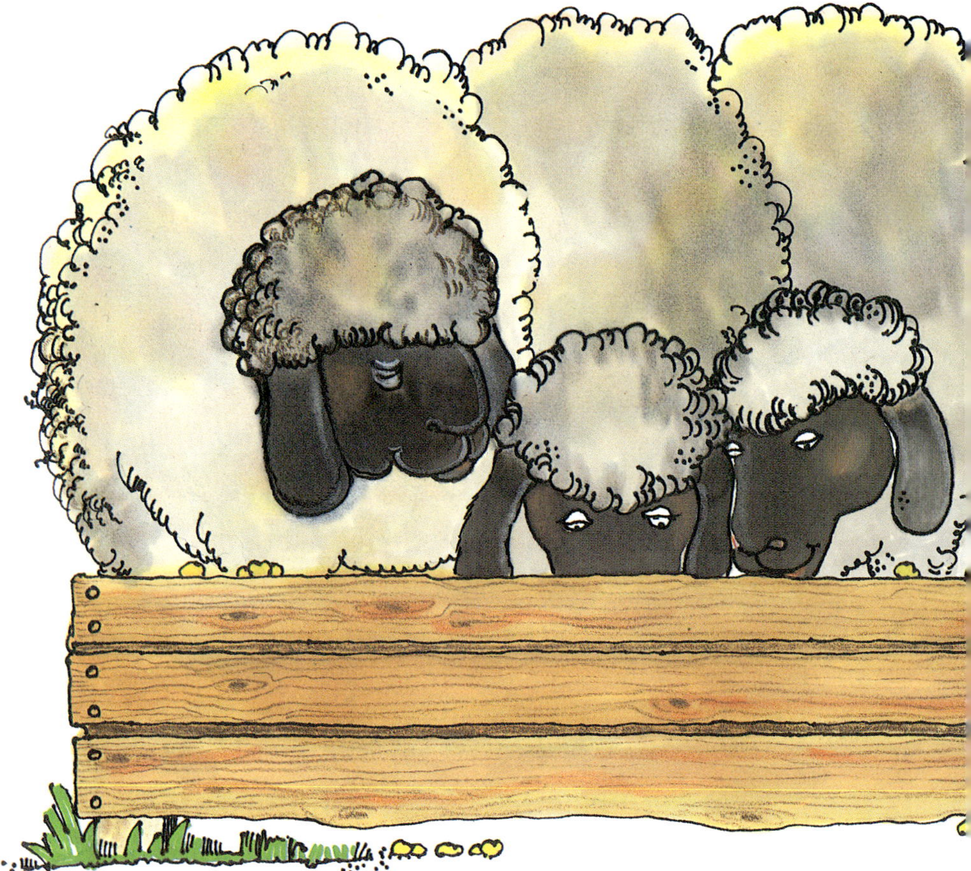

The sheep and the mice

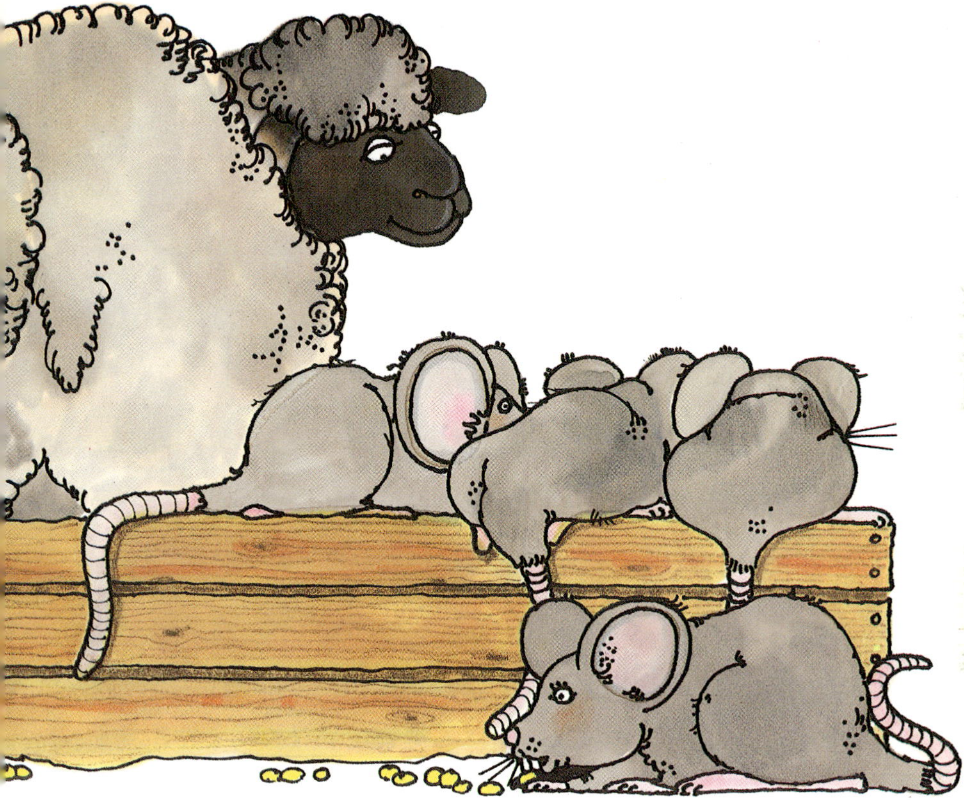

chew, chew, chew.

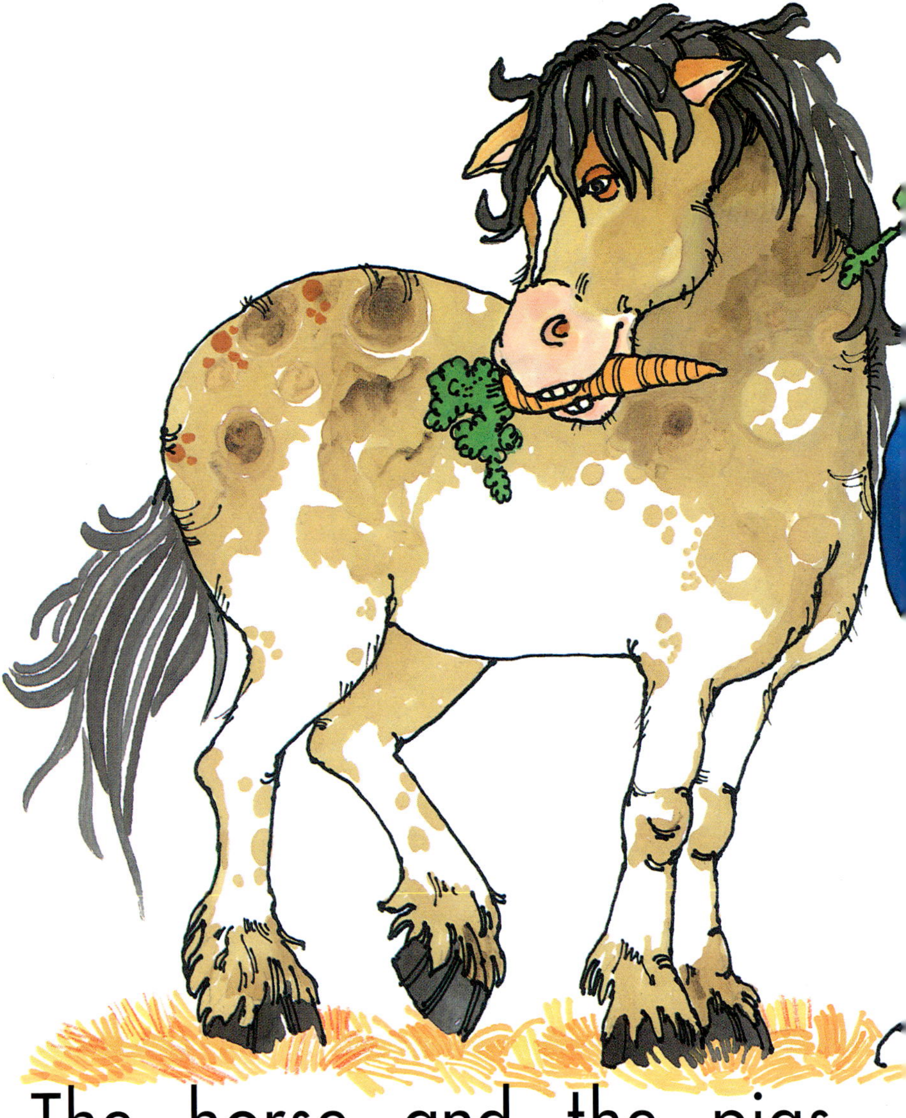

The horse and the pigs

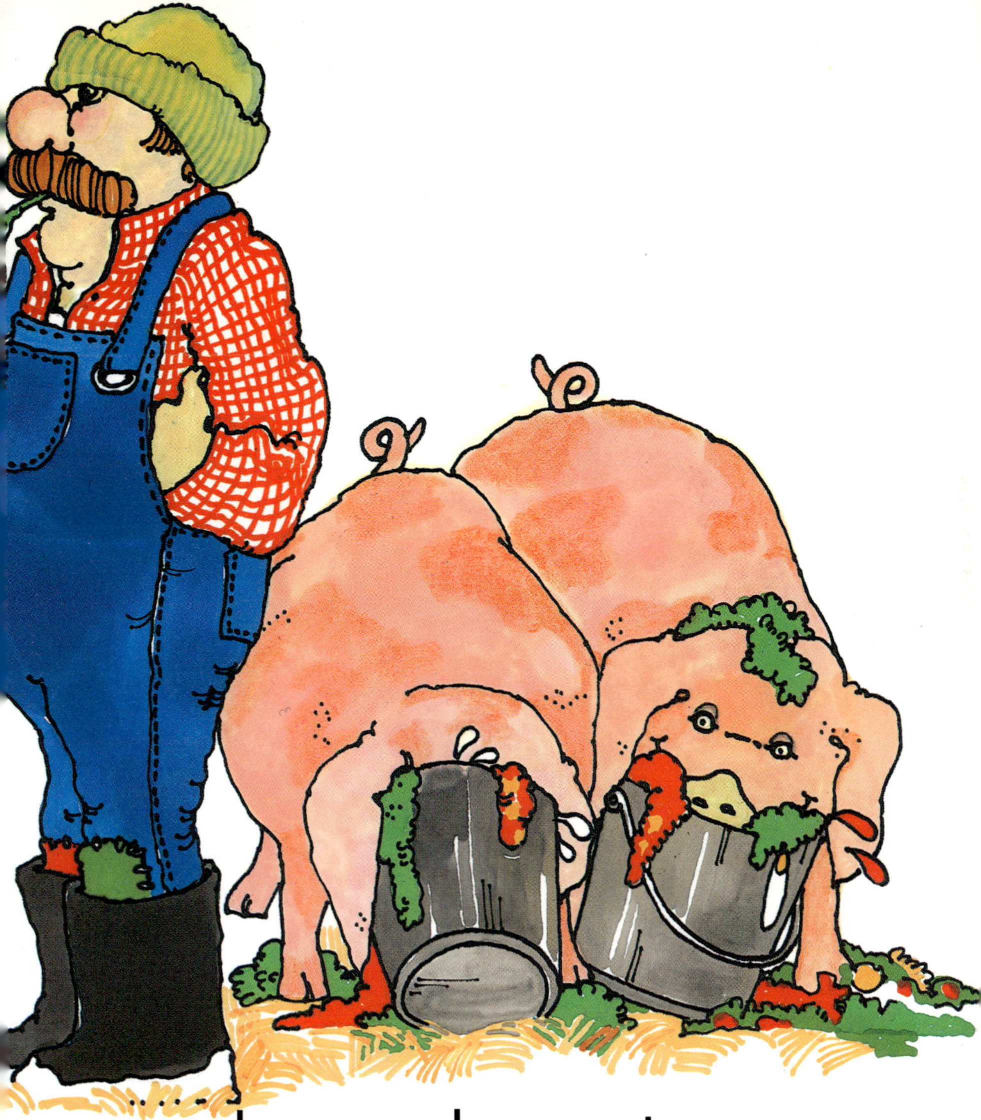

chew, chew, too.

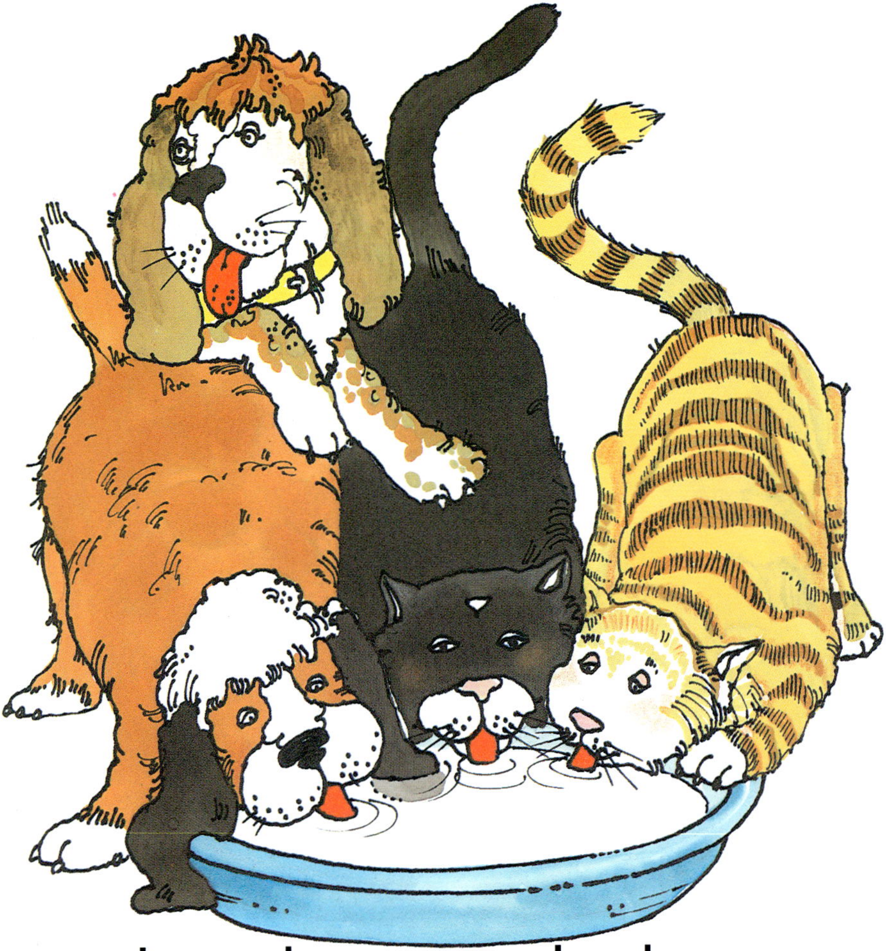

The dogs and the cats
lap, lap, lap.

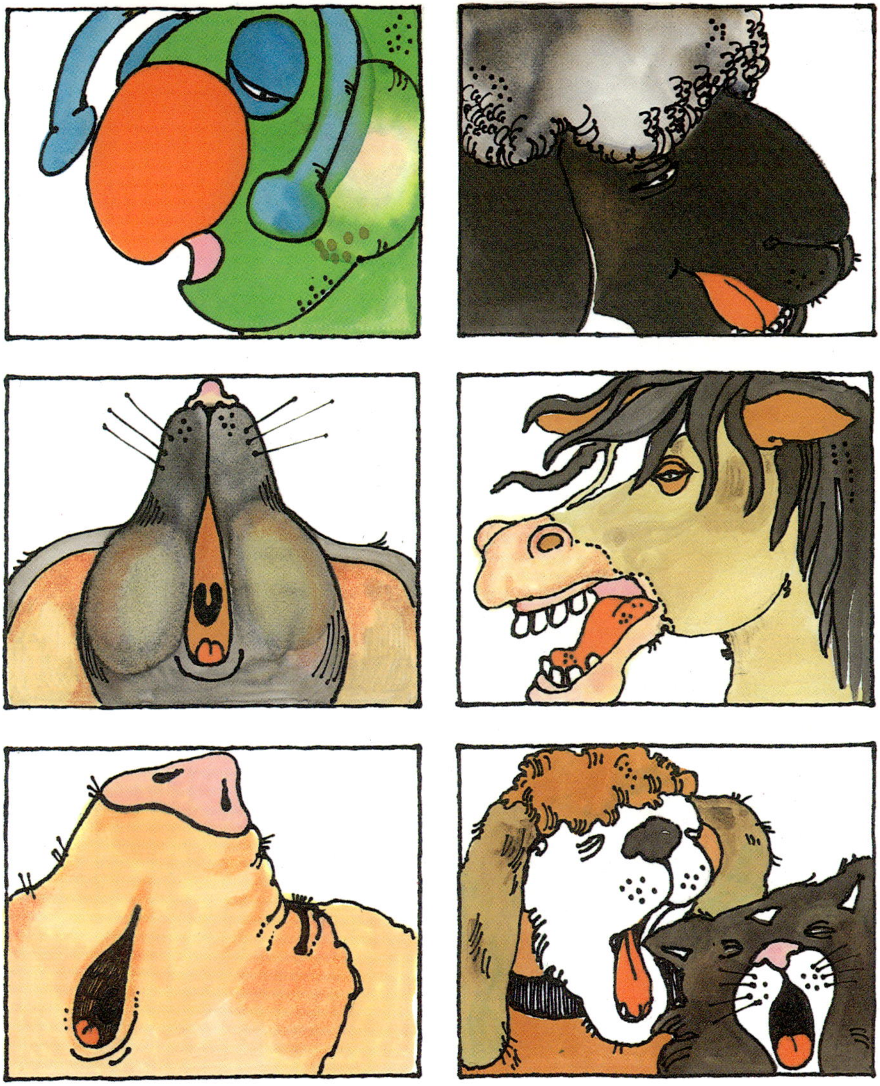

Then they all yawn...

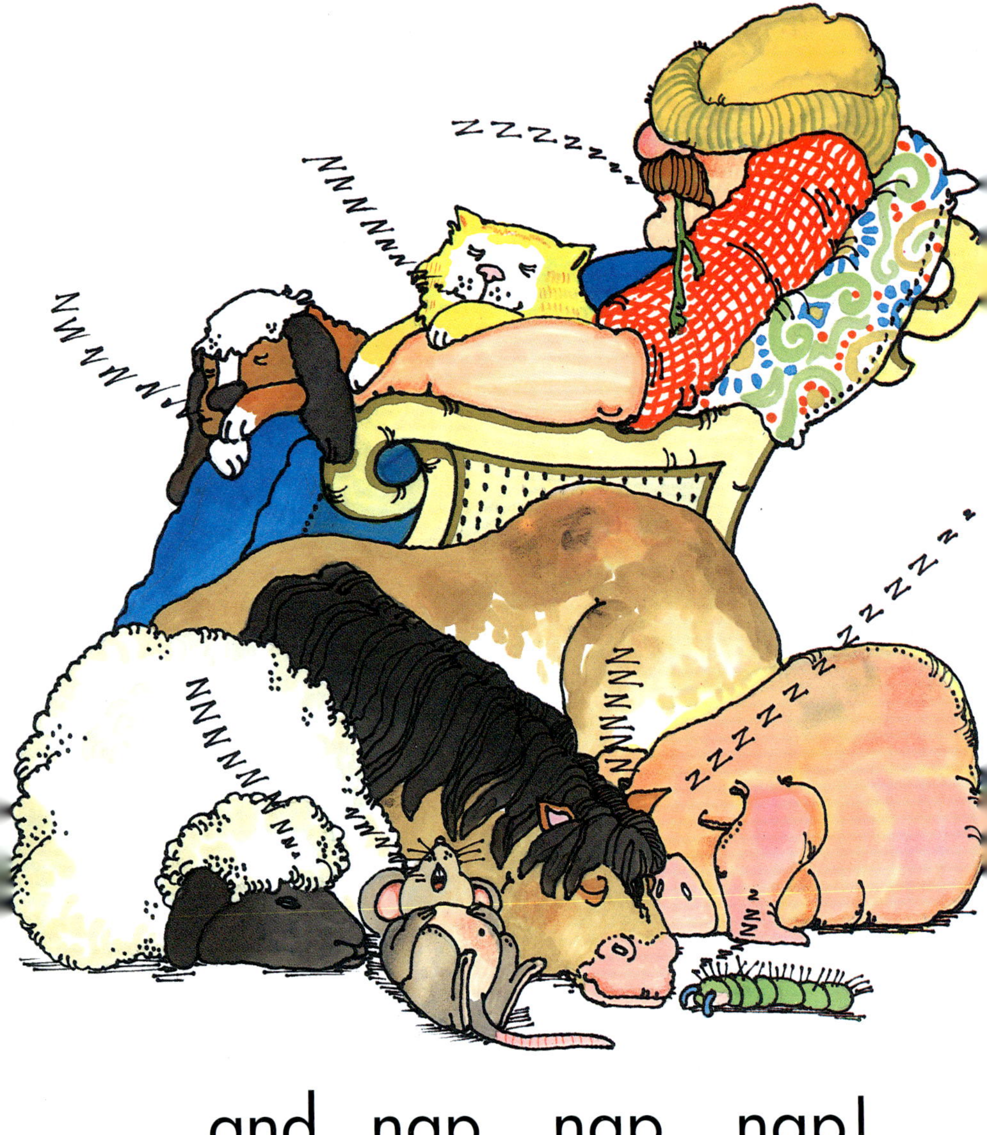

and nap, nap, nap!